EASY STEPS TO RELAXATION AND

Meditation

EASY STEPS TO RELAXATION AND

Meditation

Rosalind Widdowson

Grange
BOOKS

Published in 1995
by Grange Books
An imprint of Grange Books Plc.
The Grange
Grange Yard
London SE1 3AG

ISBN 1 85627 724 0

Printed & bound by ORIENTAL PRESS, (DUBAI).

Special Thanks

I would like to extend special thanks to my dear friend,
Chrissie Coburn-Krzowska for her invaluable help in compiling
this book. It is the first time she has shared her vast store of
knowledge in a book on meditation book. I look forward to
seeing more of her own work in print. I'd also like to give
special thanks to my partner, Stephen Marriott, who has been
so patient and hard-working and my lifelong friend Pam
Griffith, for her help in presenting this work in such an
attractive manner. Thanks also to Maria Clarke for her
loving support.

May all beings be happy and healthy.

Rosalind Widdowson

MBBO, IDTA, BWY, is a Natural Health Lifestyle Consultant.
Her work and research have taken her all over the world and
her pioneering spirit stems from a fascination with natural
health and the environment. For 30 years she has taught in a
refreshing and stimulating way and her deep-seated interests
have enabled her to develop new and imaginative ways of
teaching which have helped to establish her as one of the
leading authorities in the world.

Her interest in dance, posture, yoga, meditation, natural
healing, massage, diet and, indeed, all natural therapies was
inspired by her childhood in Africa and led to her training as
a classical dancer and teacher. Work on TV and radio started
with general health and fitness programmes.

Her writing career began in 1981 with her best-seller, 'Yoga
Made Easy'. Rosalind's busy work schedule involves running
courses at her centres in England, India, Greece and the
Caribbean. She runs her own unique teacher training course
and has networks among some of the leading natural health
organizations throughout the world.

Chrissie S. Coburn-Krzowska

CGCI, BA, BA (Hons) doctorate of Naturopathy.
Member of the Natural Medicines Society.
Full Healer, Member of the National Federation of Spiritual
Healers. Member of the World Federation of Healers.
Qualified in Reiki – Usui Shiko Ryoho System of Healing.
Trained as 'Avatar'.
Has been a natural healer since a child and a full-time
professional for the last 12 years.
Worked extensively with Native American healers. Her
Cherokee name is 'Ge-tsi-nv-si-dv'
('she who has been sent to us').
Co-Founder and Principal of Happy Home Primary School for
Tibetan Refugees, Kathmandu, Nepal.
Director (TERA) Tibetan Education Relief Association.
Founder Friends of Happy Home (FHH).
U.K. Director of FOCUS Friends' of Children United to Save
(in association with Russian International Foundation of New
Science RIFNS) which is the organization behind direct help
for people suffering the effects of Chernobyl.
Tutor of Taiji Quan, Qi Gong, Taiji Qi Gong for 15 years.
Studied in China, U.S.A. and Europe with many Chinese
and Western masters.
Studied Hatha and Raja Yoga from the age of 12 years.
Has studied in various Tibetan Buddhist Centres in Nepal,
India, Tibet and Europe for 16 years. Her Tibetan Buddhist
dharma name is 'Karma Yeshe Khandro'.
• Presently engaged in working in a Tibetan refugee centre in
the Indian Himalayas as a healer and teacher of Taiji Qi Gong.

Rosalind Widdowson

Chrissie S. Coburn-Krzowska

CONTENTS

This book represents a mere microcosm of the vast and profound corpus that is the literature of meditation. From a maze of inter-cultural and historical possibilities, a small glimpse of the variations and complexities of the human mind can be glimpsed. From one perspective, at least, meditation can be viewed as an antidote to the maladies that affect the distracted mind – as an instrument of healing. From another, it would seem that the devotional or mystical aspects of meditation are a necessary discipline, a source of inspiration and a way of offering praise to the Universal Spirit.

Even to define the word 'meditation' we need to reflect on what the word means according to the mind that apprehends it. Even the word 'mind' has a different connotation seen from the Eastern perspective. There, it is more likely to be seen as 'the intelligence of the heart' or 'heart-mind' as distinct from the Western tradition of linking the mind to the brain or intellect.

The definition of meditation ranges from systematic reflection upon religious topics, intense interior observation of our thought processes, the act of turning matters over in the mind to reach a solution or simply the desire to mentally explore the nature and purpose of the universe. The word also describes the activity of 'exercising' the mind, especially in a devotional sense. This form of meditation can mean serious and sustained reflection or mental contemplation. Its religious application is the contemplation of some religious truth, mystery or object of reverence as an exercise in piety.

According to a Christian view: "In meditation we converse with ourselves; in prayer we converse with God." However, we are also urged to recognize that the kingdom of heaven is within.

It seems to be a common view that meditation is a technique, even to be put on cassette, which involves visualization to ambient/New Age music, designed to encourage relaxation and deeper sleep. Meditation with a view towards eventual liberation from suffering, i.e. enlightenment, is a specifically spiritual perspective and is meant to 'wake us up', not to put us back to sleep. So, although there are different forms of meditation, for relaxation, life-evaluation, reprogramming (i.e. giving up smoking), these are only useful preparatory techniques, not to be confused with the ultimate aim of self-realization.

Possibly, in the context of the spiritual path, it would be more useful to say what meditation is not:

- It is not an investigation into the occult or paranormal.

- It is not a blank mind, empty of thought.

- It is not discursive thinking or introspection: it is not hypnosis, a state of suggestibility or trance.

- Rather, we need to break the spell. Meditation can de-hypnotize us and free us from all illusions and dependencies. Using methods derived from empirical techniques applied over thousands of years of human experience, we have a systematic set of techniques for studying our minds and applying discipline to the concentration and will. We will then be able to make the journey from the first layer of consciousness to explore the heights and depths. We have the spiritual technology!

If we can imagine ourselves as tadpoles, swimming around our small pool of ignorance, a person adept at meditation could be seen as a frog leaping into our world with tales of another realm. A little tadpole asks such questions as: "Well, how do you get around out there?" The frog's description of hopping and jumping would be met with blank incomprehension. "Well, it's not swimming", the frog would helpfully reply. "How do you breathe?" enquires the tadpole? The frog, getting the hang of it now, instantly replies: "Well, not with gills." "What do you breathe?" asks another. "Not water", he said enigmatically! This could continue for some time.

Ramakrishna, the Indian mystic, had this to say of knowledge; "Later, however, when the tadpole's tail of ignorance drops off, there is the ability to move between these two elements equally for full attainment of its potential."

The techniques presented in this book are continually exploring the interplay of polarities to bring us to some understanding of the harmony and balance between opposites. For us, the adventure could be to wonder if we could go all the way to heaven, embracing all, and all the way back to hell without identifying with either of them. All it needs is the capacity to be completely involved and completely detached at the same time, life's eternal paradox!

The first question that springs to mind is, "Why not?" Countless people throughout the world since time immemorial have meditated in one way or another, so it must have something going for it. It is recommended, in one form or another, by virtually every religion and belief system.

As many a regular meditator will tell you, there is a sense of 'coming home', of finding something that was precious and previously lost. Lawrence LeShan, in his book *How to Meditate* observes: "We meditate to find, to recover, to come back to something of ourselves we once dimly and unknowingly had and have lost without knowing what it was or where or when we lost it."

And what is that thing we have lost? It is contact with the full potential of our own selves that we may once have had for a short time as children, if we were lucky. To be tantalized by a thought of something better, and to later on not quite know what is missing, leads to a sense of separation and loss. We suffer, and the strongest motivation to do something about it is to alleviate it if we can.

Meditation can be seen as taking a holiday from the external world, and a journey into oneself. We all need a break now and again, and to one who meditates, that valuable time when one is truly centered within oneself, can bring refreshment to a flagging physical body, battered emotional system and overloaded mind.

It is amazing just how much time people spend on the outward search for an ecstatic union with another. It is most clearly demonstrated by the often desperate (and fruitless) search for a sexual partner to complete what is perceived as a lack in oneself. Jungians describe it as the union of our male and female selves, Animus and Anima. Whether it is acknowledged or not, most people are involved in a desperate search for 'oneness'. The object of meditation is to seek that union within, not to look for outward fixes through external distractions or other people which are

temporary measures and will not last the course. We are not talking about a heavenly 'top of the mountain' search but a very real process which brings the benefits of no longer feeling fractured, separate and cut off from the Source (however that might be imagined).

The fruits of meditation can only be realized from the practice of it. Practice can bring you to a place of surrender where a state of grace or the kingdom of heaven within can be achieved. In the external world everything is perceived as linear, measured by time. The meditative state, however, is timeless, exemplified by the statement, Be Here Now.

There are increasing numbers of people in our modern age who have rediscovered the benefits of meditation, and carers and members of the medical profession could be included in this category. On one level there is plenty of scientific research to show the value of meditation-style practices in treating conditions such as high blood pressure and anxiety. They offer a cheaper and safer alternative to drugs without the hazard of side effects. In addition, biofeedback techniques and visualization exercises are increasingly employed to help people suffering from mental disorders.

On another level, carers themselves (doctors, nurses, etc.), are appreciating the benefits meditation can bring. If, on a day-to-day basis, you are required to deal with suffering and death, there comes a point when you have to make sense of it all. If you're in a war zone it is even more difficult to reconcile your dedication to healing to the continuing carnage which surrounds you.

This need to find some underlying rationale to lives that, at some stage, may seem pointless or meaningless, will face almost everyone in the course of their lives, whatever

their occupation or lifestyle. When human beings face a personal tragedy, such as the death of a loved one, the question 'why' comes poignantly to the surface. This moment of crisis could be utilized as a point of change, a chance to transform one's life, and meditation offers, in the experience of many, the golden opportunity.

when to practise. Just do it when you feel the need for greater clarity or are at a crossroads of an important decision.

The Practice

- **Roots:** Draw the roots of the tree and don't worry if you're no great artist, that's not important. On each root fill in, either in the form of pictures, symbols or words, something that comes to mind from your childhood. It may be as trivial or as serious as you like, but be spontaneous.

- **Trunk:** Draw in a trunk and fill in the first thing that comes to mind about your adolescence, i.e. going to college, any specific training you underwent or work you undertook, any interest, friendships or relationships you formed.

- **Branches:** On each branch mark in an experience or achievement in your follow-on years, being as specific as you like.

- **Smaller Branches:** These are your dreams and aspirations, however bizarre they may be. Feel free to put down your innermost thoughts. Be honest with yourself.

- **Fruits:** These are memorable moments or occasions which you would like to record.

Now stand back and look at the general shape of the tree, roots, branches and fruit. See if there are any breaks in connection or if there is a time and place that formed a block or cut the connection with the mainstay of your life. Notice the correlation between your aspirations and your early beginnings. Study it carefully to see any visual messages it has for you. There is usually something. If there isn't, take the time and patience to come back to it at a later date and then see what it has to offer. You are not dwelling on the negative aspects of your life, you are being aware of the potential available to you in the future.

The Tree of Life

The purpose of this practice is to enable you to see more clearly where you are in the maze of your life's experiences and to evaluate the options that are open to you.

It can highlight where areas of your life are blocked, but more importantly supplies the answer to the question of where to go next along the path of helping yourself. You will need a large piece of drawing paper, a firm board to mount it on and various coloured felt tip pens. There are no rules as to where and

PREPARATION FOR RELAXATION & MEDITATION

The following are guidelines designed to help you in the initial stages of meditation. You are not required to be pure in body and mind, neither does your environment need to be wholly conducive to the practice of it. There will always be some kind of distraction such as an unplanned noise, draught, smell, etc. Do not be put off, accept it as an integral part of the meditation. Just because conditions are not always ideal you should not use this as an excuse to avoid practice!

Preparing Your Environment

It is not essential to prepare your environment for relaxation and meditation purposes. They can, in fact, be performed anywhere you feel appropriate, either going to work on the bus or in the local park, etc.

Place: In the initial stages, however, you may find it useful to practise in a special part of your home which is conducive to relaxation and meditation where you won't be disturbed. Avoid extremes of temperature and draughts though it would help to have good ventilation. Natural or subdued lighting is preferred and candlelight essential for certain practices.

You might wish to add a devotional aspect with a picture of a deity or holy person with whom you can identify. This offers a way of further expression and can act as a focal point in the practice of meditation.

Cleansing & Purification Practice

The practice of washing your body can be used as a form of ritual cleansing or purification. You can, if you choose to, think of it as a way of ridding yourself of aspects of your life that cause you distress, e.g. fear, worry, tension, fatigue, etc.

The physical benefits of scrubbing and applying lotions to the body are important. They help remove the dead cells that are constantly forming on the surface of the skin. This prevents the skin from breathing properly and leaves it feeling unnecessarily taut. If you are going to practise relaxation it is a good idea to have a warm bath or shower beforehand.

There are spiritual cleansing and purification practices which have been used throughout the centuries, e.g. sweat lodges (Native American), meditation under a waterfall (Taoist), Shanka-prakshalana (Hindu Yogic), Vajrasattva (Tibetan Buddhist), and baptism (Christian).

Preparing Your Body

Clothes: Loose-fitting natural fabrics are ideal for meditation. Both for comfort and to allow energy to flow naturally, avoid wearing belts, ties, tights, shoes, jewellery, watches or glasses.

Intake: As a general rule in life it would be best to avoid a whole range of stimulants such as coffee, tea, alcohol and recreational drugs. If you do indulge, give yourself ample time for the greater part of the effects to wear off before your practice. Ideally, do your practice in the morning before you start taking stimulating drinks.

A heavy meal before practice can cause drowsiness. Conversely, lack of food can lead to poor concentration. It is a good idea to empty your bladder and bowels before you begin and, ideally, it is best to allow two hours for a full meal to digest and half-an-hour for fluids. This might not always be possible in a busy schedule. However, even if the situation is not perfect, do your meditation practice anyway!

Physical/mental energies: If you wish to meditate first thing in the morning it is no good rolling out of bed while you're half asleep hoping to concentrate the mind. Practise some gentle stretching exercises, yogasanas, Surya Namaskar (Salute to the Sun) or Tai Chi movements to centre yourself in your physical body. You do not want your heart racing, so do nothing too strenuous or aerobic. Alternatively, take a shower to freshen up.

Conversely, if you are going to meditate when you come home from work or after a long day, chances are you will be mentally stressed or physically exhausted. This is also likely to prove a distraction. Again, perform some practices designed to unwind or de-stress the physical body and centre the concentration away from the thinking processes.

Time: It is generally recognized that there are special times that are especially auspicious and conducive to meditation; for instance, dawn and twilight, when there is a full and new moon and at the time of the equinoxes. Various cultures, from time immemorial, have recognized the special energetic potential of the interface between the opposites, light and dark, Yin and Yang, tension and relaxation. A short time before sunrise, the 'beat' or atmospheric quality of the earth seems to change. Of course, times vary depending on the country and season but experience will tell you what that 'magic time' is. Yogis refer to it as

Brahmamuhurta and it generally occurs around 4 a.m.

If possible, avoid rushing off after your practice. Take a few minutes to check for muscle cramps; massage your legs and stretch your body.

Duration: In the initial stages you needn't commit a lot of time to meditation practice. You can build up from as little as ten minutes a day. If you attempt to do too much too soon you might just be setting yourself up to fail.

Preparing Your Posture

The following are basic techniques but if you wish to carry on with advanced practices, go to a qualified teacher.

Sitting on a chair

- Sit on the front part of the chair with your hips raised above knee height (use a firm cushion if required).
- Legs should be shoulder-width apart, knees in line with the centre of the feet.

- Relax your shoulders. Do not slump, hunch or 'set' them in military fashion.

Sitting on the Floor

There are several options, e.g. a comfortable straight-backed chair is probably the easiest for most Westerners who do not habitually sit cross-legged on the floor. Sitting on a firm cushion in a cross-legged position is fine provided the hips are higher than the knees and there is no strain on the joints or spine. The distraction of aching joints for those unpractised or unfamiliar with yogic meditational postures outweighs the benefits.

Meditation postures from the yogic tradition such as Padmasana (Lotus Position) is ideal but not essential. Variations can include Ardha Padmasana (the Half Lotus), and astride kneeling position using a zafu cushion, one technique used in Japanese meditation (Zazen). The easiest technique for beginners is Sukhasana (Easy Position). Sit with the legs stretched in front of the body. Fold the right foot under the left thigh. Fold the left foot under the right thigh. Place the hands on the knees. Keep the head, neck and back straight.

The traditional meditation positions require the practitioner to sit on the floor which helps 'ground' the energy.

There are a couple of other alternatives such

s postural chairs, designed for people with bad backs (where the weight is shared by knees and buttocks) and meditation stools which relieve pressure on hip, knee and ankle joints.

Mudras:
Hand positions, in the Chair or on the Floor
The hand positions (mudras) are many and varied and are associated with specific practices which have distinct effects on the energies of the body and mind. Therefore, if you wish to go on to more complicated methods, you must study the traditions in which they are incorporated. Here are two easy methods of relaxing the hands in meditational postures:

Place your hands, palms down, on the knees.

Mudra of Equilibrium: The wrists lie on the thighs, palms upwards, left hand cradled in the right, little fingers touching the abdomen. The tips of the thumbs touch, forming a straight line, and in the space inside there is room for two eggs. In some traditions the left hand is on top of the right. In others, this is the 'male' position and the reverse is the 'female' position. In the absence of any specific tradition or instruction, use what feels most natural.

If, in the course of your meditation, the thumbs form an upward-pointing 'mountain', then there is too much tension, if a 'valley' then too little alertness. The correct position denotes equanimity.

Fine Tuning for Any Sitting Practice
Rest the tip of the tongue naturally on the upper palate on the line between the teeth and the gums. In many spiritual traditions this links the circuit of energy flowing throughout the body. It has the added advantage of slowing down the output of saliva. Continual swallowing during deep or intensive practice would be a distraction. The mouth should be closed without tension.

- If you are drowsy and in danger of nodding off, keep your eyes open. If you are agitated in any way, keep them lightly closed.

- To correct the spine, concentrate on the top of your head. Imagine a silken thread pulling the whole body upwards as though the skull were being suspended from it. Visualize the vertebrae as beads on that thread. Experience the fluidity of movement from such a viewpoint.

- On the in-breath, gently relax the muscles around the body structure, resisting the tendency to sink into the hips and slump. On the out-breath, lean the body fractionally forward. Appreciate the energetic difference.

- As a final, compassionate touch, permit yourself an inner smile.

Checking the Body Tension
Concentrate your attention on the top of the scalp.
- On the in-breath slightly tense, on the out-breath gently release the tension and allow a sensation or visualize the energy draining downwards through your body.

- Gently work your way through the body, i.e. relax facial tension, neck, shoulders, stomach or any areas of tension stored in the body.

- At the end of the practice, imagine the tension draining into the ground and discharging. The exercise can be intensified by the association of emotions connected in various areas of the body.

- To re-energize your body, breathe in, bringing the energy upwards and through the top of the head, discharging any tension.

- Reverse the procedure and breathe in energy through the top of the body and down through the body. The practice is limited only by your imagination and the time allowed.

By now your body should be in a comfortable position, relaxed and ready to approach the mind practices.

Preparing your Mind for Meditation
This is a practice for beginners who find it diffi-cult to focus their attention. It is a simple formula which can be done anywhere, anytime, either sitting up or lying in a position of relaxation.

Split-Second Formula: Think to yourself . . .

- I detach my mind from my family. I think of them and slowly detach, relax and let myself go.

- I detach my mind from my friends. I think of them, . . . detach, . . . relax, . . . and let myself go . . .

- I detach my mind from my work or chores. I think of them, . . . detach, . . . relax, . . . and let myself go.

- I hear no particular sound . . . have no particular feelings . . . time itself seems to be standing still for a split second of peace and rest . . .

Allow your mind to rest on a razor's edge between total awareness and a deep feeling of relaxation.

Stabilizing the Breath
Human beings can survive several weeks without food, several days without water, but without fresh air we are helpless. The difference between life and death is a single breath. Air contains not only oxygen but also the life force and energy from the universe (prana, Chi or Ki). We receive air through our lungs into every body cell and yet, generally, we breathe superficially, using a mere one-sixth of our lung capacity. Usually, we breathe approximately 15-20 times every minute. This usually decreases during meditation. As the body and mind relax, the breathing automatically and naturally becomes slower and deeper.

Trance states called *jhanas* are often promoted by this calming of the mind. Meditators are often warned that, although an important step, this is not the goal and can prove an obstacle to further progress. Master of meditation, Kalu Rinpoche, observed, 'at worst, tranquillity meditation is like an animal in hibernation', and suggested how this could be used. Like a 'smooth highway on which we drive to arrive at more advanced levels of Tantric meditation.' So, again, we see the vital necessity of establishing a balance between relaxation and mental alertness.

The following practice is designed to stabilize the body and mind energies through concentration on the breath.

- Without altering the breath, but simply observing it, concentrate the mind on the area below the nostrils and on the upper lip. Simply watch and feel the flow of the breath in and out of the body.

- Let the mind relax in this awareness. If thoughts arise, recognize them and let them go. If it is a 'good' or pleasant thought, be aware of the tendency to try and keep it. Recognize this habit, relax and let go. If a 'bad' thought arises, be aware of the tendency to push it away or deny it. Recognize this habit, accept the thought and simultaneously let it go. Return the mind to concentrating on the point of attention already selected. If the attention wanders, recognize the fact and without blame or judgement, gently bring the mind home. Whether the thoughts appear to be faster or slower, accept each one for what it is, another thought, and let that too dissolve.

A common misunderstanding about meditation is that we have to empty the mind. This is an impossible task, for thoughts come to the mind unbidden. For instance, If you tried to remove 'bad' reflections from a mirror or keep only the 'good' reflections you would soon realize the impossibility of the task. The nature of the mirror is to reflect everything, without grasping or refusing. Similarly, the mind can relax and be at peace within our thoughts.

"The perfect man employs his mind as a mirror, it grasps nothing, it refuses nothing, it receives but does not keep."
Chuang-Tsu

Another way of viewing this process is as a wish to find our lost peace of mind. Imagine the mind as a pool of water in which we have lost something. If we take a stick and attempt to find what we are looking for, by poking about on the bottom of the pool, all we succeed in doing is stirring up the mud and clouding the water. If we cease to disturb the water, the mud will gradually settle and the water will return to its natural state and we will be able to clearly see again. Any thought could be visualized as a stone dropping into the pool. We could watch the ripples extend from the epicentre and gradually disappear until, gradually, the water becomes as still as a mill pool reflecting an empty sky.

If we are searching for the nature of our true mind it may be helpful to regard it as our inner 'sun'. It radiates its warmth in all directions. If our thoughts are cloudy the sun may be temporarily obscured so that we forget the endless continuation of that radiance. If we attach too much importance to the clouds we may forget that the sun is always there. Our own radiant nature is always there, we simply have to let   go of all that is in the way of our understanding this.

The practice of meditation on the breath is a exercise in one-pointedness or concentration – the benefits are many including relaxation of tension of both body and mind, increased ability to concentrate on everyday matters and the clarity of mind to see situations as they truly are, increased tranquillity, acceptance of oneself and an increasing awareness of the illusory nature of thoughts.

Observations During Practice
- Watch the natural breath as it becomes shallower.

- As the inner tensions of your body relax, you may feel a wave of drowsiness. Draw yourself up out of your spine and allow the wave to flow over your head.

- If your concentration wanes you may find your thoughts dwelling on the past, in which case you may have sunk back into your pelvis. Alternatively, your thoughts may be grasping at the future and your body may well be leaning forwards. In order to bring yourself back to the present moment, simply adjust your posture so that your spine is directly in alignment with the crown of your head and you feel as if you are growing out of the base of the spine.

- Like so many of the benefits of relaxation and meditation, the effects are not necessarily evident during practice. The revitalization of body, mind and spirit can show itself in the form of healthy energy either later in the day or even the following day.

"Wear your worries like a loose robe."

It is not possible to send energy through stiff, neglected muscles, so by performing certain preparatory exercises you can help to balance the body's energies. This practice is great fun to do with a friend. It is a good example of the importance of give and take in the practice of exercise. The stretch, release and relax concept is an important one in all sound exercise programmes. Stretching movements need to be followed by periods of relaxation to allow the blood to flow through the stretched muscles. Note: If you don't have a partner try the chair exercises in **Learning How to Let Go**.

Practice

Step 1: Opposite

Sit squarely facing your partner with your knees bent, feet supporting each other, arms joined and just below shoulder level. Pause for a few rounds of breath. One partner then pulls the other towards them, holding for a few seconds. Reverse the procedure. Repeat the forward and back movements 6 times. Benefit: Eases stiff ankles, knees and hips.

Step 2: Below

The working partner places their insteps over their partner's knees. Hold hands, then arch back to maximum stretch. Hold for a few seconds and reverse the procedure to stretch forward, allowing your partner to arch their back. Repeat the forward and back stretch 6 times. Change positions to give your partner a more advanced stretch.

Step 3: Left

Press the sole of your right foot to your partner's left and stretch up diagonally forward through the arms, hands joined. Hold the stretch for a few minutes and repeat on the other side. Repeat 6 times on alternative legs.

Step 4:

Rest back to back for a few minutes to warm the muscles in the back.

Step 5:

Press the soles of both feet to your partner's and extend both your legs up between your arms, simultaneously arching them forwards and backwards, bending the knee, if necessary. Hold the balance for 2-3 minutes, gently extending your legs and spine. There are numerous variations on this theme, try to experiment (perhaps to some music) to get the rhythms of the movements more easily.

Many of our physical tensions manifest themselves in our backs. We lose more working days due to back problems than to any other complaint. The following exercises are an introduction to relaxation. They help to stretch out the tensions that form in the back muscles either side of the spinal column. They have the added advantage of strengthening the muscles which help to support the spine and prevent the problem of slipped disks.

Step 1: Left
Lie down on the floor with your legs resting on a chair. With a folded blanket under your torso, but not under the head, rest for a few minutes to allow the back muscles to 'melt' into the ground. Rest your hands just below the navel.

Step 2: Top
Hold onto the front legs of the chair and tilt it slightly back, placing your feet on either arm or on the seat. Simultaneously pull the legs of the chair to the floor while raising the hips, knees open, chin towards the chest. Keep the hips contracted but the diaphragm relaxed. Breathe naturally through the nose, allowing your chest to expand with each incoming breath. Hold for 2-3 minutes. Tilt the chair back and lower the body into the starting position by pressing the muscles of the back firmly into the ground.

Step 3: Above
Rest for 2-3 minutes with arms either above your head or in the starting position. Repeat Steps 1 – 3 several times according to your own capabilities. Ensure the chin is always at right-angles to the chest and don't clench your teeth.

Step 4: Top
Turn the chair around and tilt it to rest your legs on the diagonal. Allow the blood to flow freely down the legs. Rest for a few minutes before going on to the next step.

Step 5: Above
Push the chair legs to the floor, simultaneously pushing yourself up into the shoulder stand position. Rest your feet on the chair back, shoulder-width apart. Keep your breathing natural, your hips contracted and your diaphragm relaxed. Hold for 2-3 minutes, if possible, working up to 15 minutes when you have become more proficient. Rest for 2-3 minutes.

Note: People with high blood pressure or heart problems should only practise Step 1, 3 and 4.   **Additional Benefits:** Helps regulate the metabolism.

The best-known form of moving meditation is the sacred dance which occurs in most cultures. Many of the dances enact stories and moral tales originating from the great religions: others re-create the world of spirits, flora and fauna. Common to both is the element of meditation present in these dances which in some cases is thought to actually lead to possession. It takes years of arduous training even for the specially gifted to achieve a state of transcendence of the ordinary and the ability to inspire an audience with a sense of the divine.

It is possible to gain some concept of this type of meditation by following an exercise such as the simple re-creation of the life of a lotus. The lotus has always been a symbol of spiritual growth; it grows out of the darkness of the mud, through the medium of water to eventually bloom in air and sunlight. The *chakras* of the energetic centres of the Yogic and Tantric traditions are often referred to as lotuses. While attending to the techniques and positions of the practice, open your heart and mind to the underlying symbolism of rebirth.

> *"To see a World in a grain of sand,*
> *And a Heaven in a wild flower,*
> *Hold Infinity in the palm of your hand,*
> *And Eternity in an hour."*
>
> William Blake

The Lotus Lily
(for children and the young at heart)

This moving meditation is a practice taken from Yogarhythm. It was specifically arranged for children to give them an insight into meditation through simple visualization techniques.

Step 1:
The lotus lily starts its day in stillness...

Step 2: As the sun comes up, the petals open...and by midday its face is smiling towards the sunshine ...drawing in light and energy through its petals, through its stem to the roots.

Step 3: The gentle breeze sways the plant from one side...

Step 4: ...to the other, but always returns...

Step 5: ...to its still centre.

Step 6: There are many tiny fish swimming around in the water.

Step 7: They swim in and around the roots of the plant...

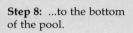

Step 8: ...to the bottom of the pool.

Step 9: There are all kinds of insects and birds...

Step 10: ... that hover overhead and come to rest on the lotus lilies.

Step 11:
The sun goes down and the petals of the lotus fold upwards...

Step 12: ... closing tightly to seal in the inspiration of the day...

Step 13: ... and rest peacefully until dawn.

DEEP RELAXATION

Yoga Nidra
Conscious Relaxation with Inner Awareness

Many leading physicians are now convinced that modern ailments and premature ageing are caused by an inability to deal with stress. Understanding and dealing with the causes is an important part of preventive treatment.

Most of us have forgotten how to relax. We once knew it instinctively as babies but gradually forgot as we became adults and the pace and pressure of modern living began to wear us down. If you have a tendency to over-interlectualize, learn to tune into the emotional and intuitive side of your nature by being more open and receptive to your heart centre. For those who consider relaxation and meditation a mere hobby or distraction, consider the basic truth underlying all spiritual practices: death is the only certainty. The moment of death is uncertain, so don't waste this precious life. This need not be a morbid preoccupation but could be used as the best reason for living our lives more usefully. To ease tension and stress is to lengthen and strengthen our lives.

The following practice, Yoga Nidra, was formulated by Paramahansa Satyananda based on the little known, but very important Tantric practice of Nyasa. The systematic rotation of consciousness can induce complete physical, mental and emotional relaxation.

Ordinarily, when you lay down to sleep and dissociate yourself from sensory input, the inclination is to fall asleep. This practice, calling for special concentration and awareness, can help you to experience that space between sleep and wakefulness. This is where contact with the subconscious and unconscious dimensions of the mind can be made.

Modern psychology calls this heightened state of sensitivity and awareness the 'hypnogogic state'. This can be a starting point from which to tackle a wonderful range of opportunities such as fast language learning. Once the process of intellectualization is bypassed, information can enter the mind which is likely to be more efficiently retained. The power of suggestion can be more effective at this time, helping us to reject distructive habits and tendencies which are causing havoc in our lives. Your true nature and integrity will come to the fore enabling you to live in peace with your environment. Yogis have used this method of introspection since time immemorial to bring them face to face with their inner selves.

The following section can be recorded on a cassette tape to enable you to establish the pattern until the sequence can be remembered and mentally repeated. Alternatively, ask a friend to guide you through the practice until you are familiar with it. Do not change the routine once the pattern has been set in the mind.

Remember, the object is to stay awake and aware throughout the practice. Do not be discouraged if you fall asleep the first few times, persevere until you can regularly achieve this state.

Yoga Nidra – the practice
Lie on your back in yoga position Savasana (Corpse Posture). Rest your arms freely by your sides, palms uppermost, arms straight but not rigid, in a natural diagonal line away from your body. Relax your fingers and let them curl naturally into the palms. Make sure your head is in alignment with your feet, legs slightly parted, feet falling open from the hips. Gently close your eyes and keep them closed. Your breathing should be natural and through your nose. There should be no physical movement during the practice.

Now is the time to make a Sankalpa (Resolution). It should be a matter of immense importance to you. A resolve is a short, positively-worded statement of intent. On one level it might be: "I resolve to take regular exercise" or "I resolve to stop smoking". On a spiritual level it might be: "I will become more aware" or "I will be kinder to all beings". It should be used regularly during your Yoga Nidra practice and should, ideally, be undertaken daily. The realization of such resolves can change your life.

Be aware of your whole body from head to toe: be completely still. Once settled into your position do not move physically.

Starting at the right thumb, repeat mentally, the name of each part of the body in the sequence outlined. As you name the body part, simultaneously become aware of it, mentally releasing and relaxing:

Right-hand thumb . . . second finger . . third finger . . . fourth finger . . . little finger . . . palm of the hand . . . back of the hand . . . wrist . . . forearm . . . elbow . . . upper arm . . . shoulder . . . armpit . . . side of the body . . . hip . . . thigh . . . knee . . . back of the knee . . . shin . . . calf . . . ankle . . . heel . . . sole . . . instep . . . big toe . . . second toe . . . third toe . . . fourth toe . . . little toe.

Become aware of the left-hand thumb . . . second finger . . .third finger . . . fourth finger . . . little finger . . . palm of the hand . . . back of the hand . . . wrist . . . forearm . . . elbow . . . upper arm . . . shoulder . . . armpit . . . side of the body . . . hip . . . thigh . . . knee . . . back of the knee . . . shin . . . calf . . . ankle . . . heel . . . sole . . . instep . . . big toe . . . second toe . . . third toe . . . fourth toe . . . little toe.

Now focus your attention on the back. Become aware of the right shoulder-blade . . . the left shoulder-blade . . . the right buttock . . . the left buttock . . . the spine . . . the whole back together.

Now focus your attention on the top of the head . . . the forehead, both sides of the head . . . the right eyebrow . . . the left eyebrow . . . the space between the eyebrows, the right eyelid, the left eyelid, the right eye, the left eye, the right ear, the left ear, the right cheek, the left cheek, the chin, the throat, the right side of the chest, the left side of the chest, the middle of the chest, the navel, the abdomen.

Now focus your attention on the right leg . . . the whole of the left leg . . . both legs together, (pause). The whole of the right arm . . . the whole of the left arm . . . both arms together, (pause). The whole of the back, buttocks, spine, shoulder-blades . . . the whole of the front, abdomen, chest . . . the whole of the back and front . . . together, . . . the whole of the head . . . the whole body together . . . the whole body together . . . the whole body together.

Repeat the process, perhaps once or twice, slowing down with each repetition.

Once your body has been stilled and you have crossed the line where you would ordinarily fall asleep you may, for the first time ever, be aware of 'who you are', existing in a state of consciousness not attached to or defined by the body. In fact, at this stage you should be scarcely aware that you have a body.

Once your awareness has been withdrawn from the senses (Pratyahara – Sense of Withdrawal) then, rather like a freshly popped bottle of champagne, your mind will be flooded with thoughts. This may be particularly true if it is the first time you have opened yourself up to this level of inner awareness.

You may perceive 'good' thoughts and 'bad' thoughts or any range of images produced by the subconscious or unconscious mind. Do not be frightened by or drawn into them. Imagine you are watching a movie displayed on a screen behind your closed eyes (Chidakasha – the Space of Consciousness). Do not be tempted to get drawn into attractive thoughts (happy memories, fantasies, etc,) or try to suppress unpleasant thoughts (negative views of yourself, feelings of anger, etc.), 'treat those two imposters just the same'. Be an observer. In time, if you continue to work with visualization or concentration techniques, the flood of thoughts will subside to a steady trickle and will eventually be only occasional visitors

This 'clearing' aspect of the Yoga Nidra technique is extremely valuable and is similar to the clearing process that goes on in the brain during REM (rapid eye movement) sleep. It is a necessary function of the human brain and therefore quite natural. The difference is that you are conscious and aware of the process. It has often been said that half-an-hour of Yoga Nidra is worth 3 hours' sleep. If you work long hours when you are denied sleep, use this technique to facilitate the necessary clearing process.

The process of Yoga Nidra ends at this point with the three-fold repetition of your resolve. Visualize your face as you see it in a mirror. See your whole body lying on the floor and, once more, become aware of the physical body. Slowly start to move your fingers and toes and stretch gently and slowly. Open your eyes and sit up.

The practice of Yoga Nidra is complete.

Since the dawn of mankind the medium of sound has, in both its sacred and profane forms, been used for healing and meditational purposes. Many of our more ancient cultures, such as pre-Christian, Chinese, Indian, Tibetan, Australian Aboriginal, Native American, South American, Polynesian, etc., have preserved the most important elements, linking sound to breath, vibration to internal organs and the chanting of 'revealed' or sacred names in paeans of praise and worship.

We are all familiar with the spectacle of sporting events enlivened by chants and songs. Singing with a choir or group is a form of group consciousness which allows the individual, for a short time, to forego their individuality and, through this temporary phenomenen, obtain a feeling of great release. This could be seen as a modern day equivalent of the pagan Saturnalia or tribal gathering. In the presence of charismatics, evangelical preachers, Pentecostal or gospel churches, the effects can be both dramatic and liberating.

In the healing arts, sounds have long been ascribed to both physical organs and their energetic, non-physical counterparts, the *chakras* (wheels/lotuses). They are amenable to manipulation by skilled practitioners and attunement through self-regulation.

The very first expressive use of musical sound by human beings almost certainly manifested itself in the drum beat. Musicians, and drummers in particular, have always known that sound and rhythm can alter human consciousness. A rhythm that mimics the heart rate will 'entrain' it. Slowly increasing the rhythm will speed up the heart to a pitch of excitement and sometimes explosive release. This technique has been cynically used by extremist political groups, for sensory pleasure at pop concerts and raves and for spiritual purposes by religious groups.

Most spiritual cultures take the view that the universe is a projection of sound vibrations alone. Muslim (Sufi) saints have said that the world evolved from sound and form and the Bible states: "In the beginning was the Word (sound), and the Word was with God and the Word was God." Modern science concurs that everything in the universe is nothing more than the continual interplay of vibrational energy and sound is no more than a particular form of vibration. As Paramahansa Satyananda points out: "Yoga philosophy maintains that even the different layers of mind and body, gross and subtle, are nothing but the manifestation of an uncountable number of different sound vibrations in a multitude of permutations and combinations. We can say that the mind and the body are the solidification of sound."

The Name Of God

Every culture has a name for God as the Supreme Ground of Consciousness or Love or Awareness, however the Divine is described. These names are sometimes 'revealed' to saints, sages, holy men, prophets and shamans (native healers) who have directly experienced them in superconscious states. The Yogic and Tantric traditions maintain that the names of God are the nearest vocal equivalent to a much more subtle sound. By the repetition and chanting of names such as Jesus Christ, Rama, Krishna and Shiva, Allah, etc., one can bring one's consciousness into sympathetic resonance with the divine energies. What initially start out as vocal sounds are eventually interpreted by the mind in a far more subtle way. Rather like cranking up a generator or winding up a spinning top, the momentum will start to carry the practitioner along. This leads to identification with the divine and, sometimes, to expression of those qualities associated with it.

Hymn singing is the most obvious Christian practice while repetition of the Koran (Muslim) or the Bhagavad Gita (Hindu) are both well-known and respected practices.

The Mantra

A mantra is a potent sound or series of sounds which are used to induce an altered state of consciousness. The word 'mantra' is from the Sanskrit noun *manas* which pertains to mind in conjunction with the verb root *tra,* meaning to protect. Simple repetitions of mantras, while going about one's everyday tasks, protect the mind from wandering and disturbing thoughts. This is especially efficacious when used in conjunction with rosary beads, prayer or worry beads and malas where physical and vocal repetition is combined.

On another level, mantras can be used as energetic tools, potent symbols that can be used to shock, calm and stimulate energetic blocks within oneself or others. This requires a high level of understanding and experience and would usually be used by a spiritual teacher or a prepared pupil, a healer on a patient or a martial artist on an opponent (the famed Japanese 'Kiai' that can momentarily paralyse) Conversely, from the same tradition, meditation is vital to truly understand that silence is a prerequisite before the mind and body can recover their natural unity.

"Out of silence rises up Immortal Spirit."
In the same way that movement comes from stillness, the cry of the spirit rises out of silence.

Meditational Practice
Aum or Om Chanting
OM MANI PADME HUM is one of the best known of mantras, commonly translated as 'Precious Jewel in the Lotus' and often referred to as the Mantra of Compassion in the Buddhist tradition. It has many uses ranging from a simple method of protection for the mind to a spiritual dynamic producing profound insights into outer, inner and supreme realizations. 'OM', in this context, represents the body and externally purified negative actions. Internally, it purifies all perceptions and the subtle channels. The depth of knowledge involved in even one such mantra is vast and a subject worthy of study in its own right.

Instruction from a teacher of recognized provenance and experience is necessary if you wish to use visualization to realize the full potential of the mantra. However, you will be able to gain some first-hand experience by practising the following technique.

Chant the mantra OM or, more correctly, AUM. This sacred sound is universally recognized as a beneficial resonance. It recurs in the main religions, to Jews and Christians as 'Amen', to Muslims as 'Amin' and to Hindus and Buddhists as 'Aum'. It is the most fundamental of sounds reproduced by the human voice when exhaling from abdomen, rib cage and chest in a complete breath.

- Inhale, expanding first the abdomen to draw air deep into the lungs. As you continue inhaling, the rib cage expands and finally you fill the chest.

- Exhale slowly by contracting the abdomen and sounding the syllable Aaaaaaaaaaaa. As you contract the rib cage the sound should change to Oooooo. Finally there should be a trailing off of resonance in the upper chest and resonance in the nasal cavities of Mmmmmm. The three sounds should gently merge one into the other – AaaaaaOoooooOMmmmmmm.

- Repeat as many times as you wish.

Kirtan

Kirtan is a form of devotional singing using mantras which contain the names of God. The most familiar is likely to be the Maha Mantra (Great Mantra) of Hare Krishna, Hare Krishna, Krishna Krishna, Hare Hare, Hare Rama, Hare Rama, Rama Rama, Hare Hare. Om Namah Shivaya and its variations are also very well known. Repetition with the mind and heart on the object of one's devotion is the key to this process. Singing, drumming with mridanga and tabla, and the hand-pumped harmonium are the traditional instruments which accompany this form of devotional practice.

Nada Yoga
'The Flow of Consciousness' – Sound

Nada Yoga originates from the Yogic, Tantric and Sufic traditions which are part of a world-wide spiritual culture, not specifically confined to one location, religion or belief system. The following techniques are methods of penetrating the deeper layers of the mind using sound as a medium. They are excellent practices for inducing Pratyahara (Sense of Withdrawal) and states of meditation.

They will calm and de-stress an overactive, overtaxed or worried mind.

There is a theory that every individual body produces its own unique sound. If we allow ourselves to experiment with subtle sound it offers a way to become attuned and in harmony with the natural vibrations of our body, speech and mind.

Beginners should practise in a place and at a time when external sounds are at a minimum. Late at night or early in the morning are especially recommended. There is no set duration for this practice although 15 minutes is the minimum to gain any effect. Regularity of practice is the key to fruitful experience.

Bhramari Pranayama –
Humming Bee Breathing

- Sit comfortably, in a chair or on the floor, with your head, neck and spine in a straight line. Let your breathing be relaxed, calm and natural.

- Inhale, tuck your chin into your neck and hold the breath for as long as is quite comfortable.

- Raise your chin, gently close your ears with your fingers, and exhale with a continuous, unforced humming note. You will feel a very pleasant vibration in your head and chest.

- Repeat for as many breaths as you wish. Sit quietly after your practice and listen for the subtle reverberations.

Meditational practice:
Nada Yoga

- Squat on a rolled-up blanket or large cushion, keeping this beneath the buttocks and between the legs. The cushion should be high enough so that the back is not cramped. Rest your elbows on your knees, place your fingers on the top of your head and seal the ears gently with the thumbs.

- Relax the whole body. Keep the teeth slightly separated and the mouth closed.

- Inhale deeply and while exhaling, produce a humming sound like a bee. Feel it vibrate throughout the head starting from the base of the throat (5 minutes).

- Stop humming and listen for subtle sounds. Keep listening for any sound. One will become clearer and clearer. Keep your mind totally on this sound. Listen with intensity.
- As your hearing ability becomes more sensitive you will be able to detect another sound in the background, behind the predominant one.

- Leave the first sound and concentrate on the emerging sound. Eventually you will be able to hear yet another sound behind the second. Again concentrate on this third sound and bring it to the fore.

- Carry on in this manner, searching for ever more subtle sounds. The more subtle the sound, the deeper you delve into the mind.

Don't be discouraged if you can't hear the subtle sounds at first, practice and attunement may take time. The sounds you may perceive depend very much on your personality and cultural background since so much is a relative interpretation. When outer sounds and inner sounds cease to distract, we find a paradox emerging, described in the Buddhist tradition as *'The Roaring Silence'*.

Chun Fu / Inner Truth

This symbol, shown on the wall in the picture on the left, expresses the truth and origins of spirituality. In the figure, two broken lines (Yin-feminine) lie between two solid lines (Yang-masculine). This denotes emptiness within form and represents a pure, open and empty mind, a heart free of prejudice and therefore open to truth.

Joyousness and gentleness are the attributes of two primal trigrams: *Tui* means joyousness in following the good and *Sun* means penetrating into the hearts of men.

"...Inner Truth and Perseverence to further one. Thus man is in accord with heaven."

"I Ching" translated by Richard Wilhelm

**"Be still as a mountain,
move like a river."**

Body awareness is one of the first steps in the practice of relaxation. Muscles automatically relax when the mind is resting and the emotions stilled.

It is possible for a great deal of energy to drain away if you don't have periods of relaxation. By conserving energy, the body and mind can achieve a state of tranquillity and serenity.

It is easy to become accustomed to the fact that one is lacking in energy and in a perpetual state of nervous agitation. This causes blood vessels to contract, hampering the release of impurities from the body and increases susceptibility to disease or illness. Relaxation is truly the elixir of life. The various methods enable you to meet each day with the spirit of a mild spring breeze rather than that of a whirlwind. By regular practice you will be able to naturally balance any tendencies towards depression, anxiety or over-excitement in your daily life.

To live in a state of tranquillity can be compared to the calm, still surface of the water reflecting the moon and a flying bird. It neither grasps the one nor rejects the other. True living calm is the mind that reflects with equanimity.

Standing Practices
(to help calm the mind and steady the body)

Basic Stance
(standing in a natural and relaxed posture)

Unlike Yoga, Tai Chi Ch'uan is performed with the body upright (Basic Stance for many martial arts).

- Stand with your feet parallel, shoulder-width apart, with the weight equally distributed. The skeleton hangs as though suspended from the crown of the head.

- Relax through the joints so that the body's weight sinks downwards and 'roots' through the feet.

- Allow your arms to hang freely by your sides.

- Stand quietly, breathing naturally and allow the body to recognize its connection to the earth.

- Rest the tongue on the line between the upper teeth and the palate. Relax the face in a subtle inner smile.

Waterfall Meditation
(for purifying the body and mind)

Imagine you are standing under a waterfall. A stream of water gently cascades over your head, running downwards over the outside of your body, taking with it tensions and negativities. These soak harmlessly into the ground.
Repeat three times.
Imagine that the water is entering the crown of the head (bai hui), and its cleansing force is running through the inside of your body. Use your imagination to visualize the cleansing of the organs, joints, digestive tract, etc. The water drains the negativities and toxins out of the body which pass through the soles of the feet and into the earth.

Note: The temperature of the water can be imagined as hot, cold or warm, depending on the climate and whether you are feeling over- or under-stimulated.

Meditation with the Breath
(for unifying our energy with the universe)

The universe is a limitless circle with a limitless radius. Condense this into One Point and centre it on the lower T'antien (Field of Immortality) which is the centre of our universe.

To find this centre, adopt Basic Stance as before, with the first three fingers of the left hand underneath the navel. Take the index finger of the right hand, place it in line with the navel, underneath the fingers, pointing towards the spine. Imagine a small sphere of condensed energy resting just in front of the spine.

This is the physical centre of the body's gravity and also the meeting point of ascending energy from the earth (Yin) and descending energy from the sky (Yang). The dynamic interplay of the 'marriage of opposites', is the internal alchemical marriage of the male/female energies of the universe. This is the source of the vital energy which keeps the practitioner healthy and leads to an extended, useful life.

In Taoism, the inspiration for practice comes from the belief that we have evolved sufficiently to need but one human rebirth. The ultimate

'attainment' is to become 'an Immortal', one who has transcended birth and death. In Hinduism and Buddhism the theory of reincarnation states that a dedicated enough follower can be released from the cycle of birth, death and rebirth in one lifetime. Those of lesser achievement can work towards a future rebirth and in the process receive more support, i.e. a strong body, supportive parents, access to spiritual teachings, etc.

Many of the various martial/spiritual disciplines from the East contain a synthesis of Taoist/Buddhist/Confucianist beliefs. The 'long life' practices which spring from the Taoist viewpoint that we should make the best use of this precious opportunity that is human life, affords the best chance of realization. Free from the distractions of ill health and motivated by this premise we can endeavour to gain insight into the age-old questions of "Who Am I? Where did I come from? Why am I here and where am I going?" Many of the mind techniques in advanced practices deal with this question from the viewpoint of "Who is this I?"

The Practice

- Relax into Basic Stance. Breathe naturally for a few moments.

- Extend the out-breath so that it travels infinitely to the ends of the universe.

- Breathe in so that your breath reaches your One Point (T'antien) and continues infinitely.

- Repeat for at least 5 minutes and no longer than 15 minutes initially. Increase at your own discretion.

This Chi breathing method is a simple and important way of unifying mind and body.

- At night, when all is quiet and calm, do this alone and you will feel that you are the universe and the universe is you.

Benefits
You will be led to the Supreme Ecstasy of being One with the Universe. At this moment, the life power that is rightfully yours is fully activated.
(With acknowledgement to the Ki sayings of Koichi Tohei, Aikido Master.)

Moving Meditation
The method of Tai Chi Ch'uan originates from, and is generated by stillness.

"The mind should come first and the body later."

"The body should follow the mind as a shadow follows an object."

"All movements are directed by the mind, not by exerting muscular strength."

These quotes from the masters show the importance of a concentrated mind in a relaxed body.

To say 'relax' is to poorly translate the often repeated Chinese command, *Sung*. A Chinese Master, at a loss to communicate this instruction to his pupils, dropped all attempts at verbal explanation and mimed the following: He pretended to take an imaginary piece of heavy elastic between his hands. Grunting and straining, he pulled his hands about a foot apart. Eyes bulging and breathing heavily, he maintained this grip for a few moments. With a relieved sigh he then slowly relinquished his stretching with the words: "Sung, Sung," as his hands relaxed back to the original position. From his point of view, most Westerners carry this amount of tension with them without any real awareness of its presence. Relaxation is therefore a natural state to which we can return, not one which we need to acquire. Hence, the frequently-heard 'investment in loss' while learning Tai Chi Ch'uan.

It is impossible to give a description and teaching of the moving Tai Chi form in this book. The following exercise will, however, give a taste of the feeling of movement originating not from muscular force, but from internal energy combining breathing and thought.

The paradox, 'effortless effort', is experienced by cultivating a continual letting go and surrender of ego and the giving up of unwanted tension.

From the pages of the *Tao Te Ching* comes this description of the philosophy of Wu Wei on the subject of non-action:

"Less and less is done until non-action is achieved. When nothing is done, nothing is left undone. The world is ruled by letting things take their course. It cannot be ruled by interfering."

This is the antithesis of the attitude expressed in our scientific, technological society. The Way of Tao is to harmonize with the forces of Nature, not to conquer them. Meditation provides us with an opportunity to listen, in quietness, to our innate, natural saneness – an alternative to our tendency to control our 'body-vehicles' rather than working in friendship with our physical being.

A Taste of Tai Chi Ch'uan

- Stand in Basic Stance (as previous exercise).

- Close your eyes, concentrating on the breath, allowing it to naturally slow down and deepen.

- Extend your awareness to include the whole body.

- On the in-breath, imagine the breath filling the whole body.

- On the out-breath, imagine the body emptying.

- On each exhalation, feel your hands and arms swell out and float away from the sides of your body.

At first, the movements are subtle and small, but as the practice progresses the feeling is that they are effortless and come from the inside out. This is the physical embodiment of Wu Wei's teaching, non-acting, non-doing. The unification of body and breath rises and falls like the natural rhythm of a calm ocean.

- You can extend this movement gradually, breathing in as you raise the arms and out as you relax them down by your sides.

Concentrate your mind entirely on the sensation of 'allowing' the arms to float upwards, assisted by the breath. Allow them to relax and respond to the gravitational pull on the out-breath. Experience the willingness of the body to follow the gentle guidance of the mind.

Contrast this with the unaware actions of our everyday movements. The brain/mind orders the vehicle of the body around, often with little regard to its innate intelligence. With a spirit of friendly co-operation between mind and body the 'enemy within' has been recognized and embraced. This is the beginning of the wisdom of 'martial heart' activity and the beginnings of compassion!

The arrogance of the intellect is one of the greatest enemies of the martial artist. In the Eastern system of grading, the white belt denotes the student beginner. He or she then rises through the ranks eventually gaining the prized black belt. After attaining further grades, the Master once more wears the white belt. This exercise in humility is reflected in the saying: "Zen Mind, Beginner's Mind".

If you have come to this book and these practices, thinking: "I can't do these meditations, I'm just a beginner," be thankful. This is the most useful approach even if you're an expert!

These methods are useful for concentrating the mind to a focus of single-pointedness. Imagine the sun's rays caught by a magnifying glass. Think of the effect of the concentration of these rays onto a point on a piece of paper. After a time, the paper will scorch and finally burst into flames. When the mind is supremely focused, who knows to what extent latent power can be realized.

There are two main methods, the external or 'object of meditation' and the internal, focus, image or visualization.

External Practices Using an Object

Many objects are classically used for meditational purposes: depending on the system of belief, culture and intention, these can vary immensely. An object of religious contemplation can be used as a means of channelling concentration, such as the elaborate iconographical representations of different aspects of consciousness. These can include the pantheon of deities or avatars of Eastern systems (as well as those associated with Christianity) together with the simple geometric representations (*yantra*) of cosmic forces. The image may represent the embodiment of an abstract quality such as Compassion (Chen Rezig) in a Tibetan Buddhist t'ankha (painting) which can be used as a Tantric meditational device to 'realize the emptiness of all phenomena'. Whatever object of meditation is used and from whatever culture, it is still possible to reach a common goal even if they are along different routes of understanding. Depending on form and colour, different images can evoke varying changes of consciousness and states of awareness in the mind of the practitioner.

Other objects that can be included in this meditation: a flower, a stone, everyday object, a living candle flame, moving water (the latter two a little more difficult). In the advanced practices of Dzogchen, the gaze rests in the Infinite Space of the Sky, the most subtle external object.

Candle Meditation
Trataka
"There is a healing light shining in the centre of my being."

The word *Trataka* means to gaze steadily. It is one of the best-known practices to develop power of concentration and memory. It has the additional benefit of strengthening eye muscles, thus improving eyesight.

Practice

- Sit comfortably either on the floor or in a chair (see Preparations for Relaxation & Meditation).

- Place a candle at arm's length and at eye level, directly in front of the body when in a sitting position, and light it.

- Close your eyes and become aware of the whole body. Make any necessary adjustments so that you will not need to move during the practice.

- Open your eyes and gaze at the brightest part of the flame, just above the wick. Your eyes should be wide open, though without strain. Try not to blink if you can help it. With practice this will get easier but if you feel real discomfort, blink gently, then continue with your practice. Do not move the pupils.

- If your mind wanders, gently bring it back. Do this for 3 minutes then close your eyes. Visualize the after-image of the candle flame at the centre between the eyebrows (Bhrumadhya).

- Practise for as long as the image is clear. If any thoughts arise then simply be a witness to them.

- Open your eyes again and focus on the candle flame for about 3 minutes.

- Close your eyes again and concentrate on the inner image.

- Repeat this process of outer gaze and inner visualization for as long as you wish. Finally, keep your eyes closed and be a witness to your thoughts. Open your eyes and extinguish the candle.

An alternative way of using an object for meditational practice is to use it simply as a reference point in order to witness or observe the way the mind reacts when focused upon it. The following practice is a starting point to exercise the mind. In the same way that a physical work-out in a gymnasium (if done skilfully) can strengthen the body and increase flexibility, these mind practices will enable the mind to be stretched and focused. It is important to avoid indulging in mere 'mental gymnastics' but to proceed with a clear understanding of our motivation.

These are preparations to loosen up the tensions of habitual mind patterns that may not be serving us usefully. A well-balanced work-out should have the result of healthily relaxing our body or mind (preferably a synthesis of both).

Meditation Practices
"The Great Square Has No Corners."
This is a quotation from a well-known and respected text called the *Tao Te Ching*, a 6th century Chinese classic by Lao Tsu. To describe the philosophy of The Tao (The Way) is a virtually impossible task. Consider the following: "The Tao which can be told is not the eternal Tao. The Name that can be Named is not the Eternal Name." You can see the problem!

This paradox is also echoed in the Native American view of Wakan Tanka, originally translated as 'Great White Spirit' or even more simply 'Great Spirit'. The more profound and accurate translation is 'Great Mystery', leading us again and again to the futility of trying to express the inexpressible. What can we learn from this? Maybe that an ordinary or finite consciousness attempting to name the Infinite can only point a finger along the Path. The real understanding is to be found alone and in silence. Therefore, any meditational device could be seen as a trick to trap the unwary ego into letting go its death grip on the True Mind.

With this in 'mind', the following practice could be provoking.

Practice
"The Great Square Has No Corners."
Contemplate this simple sentence.
Sit in a comfortable meditational posture, close the eyes and, with relaxed breath, repeat this phrase a few times, focusing your attention on it and observing what arises. It can be done either audibly or silently.

This could be viewed as an internal focus of attention. Whatever arises, simply accept and move on.

Practice
"The Great Square Has No Corners."
Meditation on an external object

- On a piece of plain white card, draw an outline of a square in black. Make it whatever size you feel is appropriate for an object of contemplation. Experience the physical creation of this shape. Drawing can be a meditation exercise in its own right. Try to execute the drawing with efficiency and give it your full attention.

- Sit in a comfortable meditational position with the drawing at eye level.

- Do whatever relaxation procedures you find useful.

- Concentrate on resting your gaze on the image. Breathe naturally.

- Let your attention explore the edges without losing attention or letting the mind wander. Allow approximately 10 minutes.

This practice can also be used with alternative objects for meditation. Observe the difference when there is already an attachment to the object used as opposed to a more randomly-selected one. At the end of the session accept whatever experience has arisen as a mere thought. Relax and let go.

Meditation on an Internal Object

- Continue this practice with the eyes closed. Re-create or bring to mind the square image. There may be some image distortions which are purely physiological due to the retention of the image on the retina, but do not let this distract you.

- Bring to mind the phrase "The Great Square Has No Corners" and continue to visualize the square.

- Explore the limits of the square and gradually expand your awareness to the furthest limits and see what happens. If your attention wanders or if you are not satisfied with the result (whatever it may be), bring the mind back to the square and start again. Allow approximately 10 minutes.

Some Possible Reviews
If the square image was enlarged to the greatest possible extent it may, eventually, lose its corners and become a circle. This is one way of viewing this mysterious paradigm.

- Try this meditation once more, placing yourself at the centre of a cube. Expand the six square sides outwards and watch what happens. In three dimensions, the cube becomes a sphere. This, too, can be expanded in all directions as far as your mind is able to conceive. Fully engage yourself in feeling this experience.

- Rest in this space.

This resting of the mind into spaciousness, without grasping at it or rejecting it, enables the meditator to achieve a sense of 'timelesness' in a fourth dimension (time).

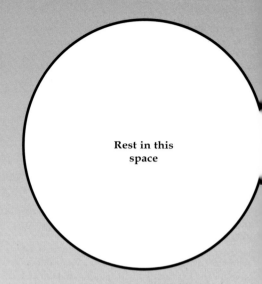

Rest in this space

More Possible Reviews
The square (also the cruciform) is an archetype denoting the Earth. The perfect square only exists as a concept. It does not appear in nature. The closest is the rhomboid shapes of inert, crystalline structures. It could be said that the square represents the conceptual or finite vision and, when expanded to the infinite, becomes the circle. This could be the inner meaning of the medieval alchemist's preoccupation with the 'squaring of the circle'. So, in summary, the square Earth is transcended by the circle of heaven and the infinite contains the finite. The paradox is that within our finite body form we are able, with the help of the mind, to experience the infinite spaciousness of expanded consciousness.

Note: In the meditation each experience of a limitation should be accepted and released as, 'just a thought'. This then becomes an on-going practice and your limitations are no longer obstacles but merely the parameters of your mind.

A Few Useful Notes
Once you set a format up, such as the previous meditation, remember that you chose to do it and that it is helpful for you to recognize your commitment.

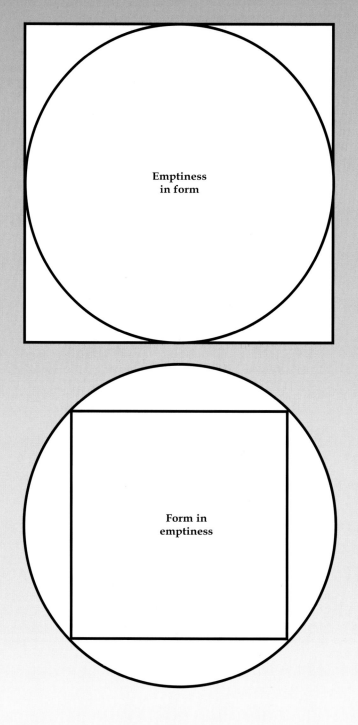

Emptiness in form

Form in emptiness

For example, these following ideas may have been part of your meditational experience:

- A feeling of joy or bliss, followed by: *"I've got it, I've got it!"*

- A feeling of fear, followed by: *"I've lost it, I've lost it!"*
- A feeling of envy, followed by: *"He/she has got it, and I haven't!"*

- A feeling of boredom, followed by: *"I don't care anyway!"*

- A feeling of doubt, followed by: *"I don't know if I'm doing this right!"*

Maybe you recognize one or more of these? The list is endless. Maybe you had a unique thought of your own. However, realize that what they are is not important, individually. Just realize that they are simply thoughts and therefore distractions. Any attachment to, or rejection of them is limiting you. So, find it, recognize it, accept it. This is your 'edge' or limitation. Without the flight or fight reaction, allow yourself to experience this boundary and relax the mind in order to expand it. You can then continue the practice without losing concentration or having to return to the beginning of the technique. In this way, you can enable yourself to handle what could have been an obstacle to your meditation and transform it into part of your practice.

Things To Do

Recognize your insights and:

- enjoy them

- record/write them down, satisfy your need to express. Recognize also that even these creative pursuits are still distractions from the actual practice of meditation. So . . .

DO IT AGAIN!

MEDITATIVE WALKING

It is essential that one learns to take a state of consciousness achieved through a sitting meditation out into the world. It will remind you that a meditative state is not a rare and exotic flower which only blooms in the hothouse of esoteric meditational practice. Ideally, the meditative state should be part of your everyday life. Even when doing the most mundane tasks, you should endeavour to bring a quality of meditation to it. The famous Chinese and Japanese tea ceremonies are important rituals as well as forms of spiritual meditation. They are ways of bringing full awareness to a simple, everyday task that we all perform, a lesson in extracting enjoyment from anything and everything and living fully in the moment.

One of the best places to start is your first walk outside of the meditational environment. Following your practice, and while still in a mood of concentrated awareness, go for a walk. Bring to bear all the aspects which you have just be practising. Walk purposefully and maintain a quiet, alert mind. Concentrate the mind without tension.

Da Liu, author of *T'ai Chi Ch'uan and Meditation* makes the suggestion: "Walk with the body erect, the shoulders relaxed, and the elbow and knee joints loose. . . . Direct the bulk of your weight below the navel. The foot touching the ground should bear the brunt of your weight, while the other foot remains light and weightless."

In order to allow the toes and feet to move naturally, bare feet or soft comfortable shoes such as Tai Chi slippers are ideal. The action of placing the whole of the foot (sole, heel and toes) with awareness, acts in the same way as reflexology, increasing the ordinary stimulating effect on the meridians (energy points) as well as veins, glands, nerves, etc.

Notice the action of lifting one foot and placing it in front of you. Be aware of the shift in the body's weight, the contracting and releasing of muscle groups, of balance, of the resistance of the ground to your feet, of heat and cold, of flexibility and inflexibility. Notice your 'intention' – your intention to make a movement before you make it.

Lift, push, place, lift, push, place, lift, push, place. After practising this technique for the first time young monks often report back to their superiors a whole range of exciting discoveries and insights. They are always told simply: "Return to your practice." Lift, push, place. It can get even more subtle than that with: intention to lift, lift, intention to push, push, intention to place, place.

Note: Because of the subtle energies involved in this practice, avoid plastic soles on footwear and walking on concrete. These unnatural materials have the effect of making sluggish the flow of energy from earth to body.

TONG-LEN MEDITATION

Taking and Giving: Root Practice for Eradicating Suffering

Loving 'oneself' as an act of enlightened self-interest, not as selfishness.

This meditation is from the Tibetan Buddhist tradition and engenders compassion by means of taking the suffering of others and replacing it with the gift of our own happiness. The practice concentrates on the specific nature of the thoughts we have in relation to other people. They can cause us distress of the mind, distress of the emotions and distress of the body. It helps to develop kindness to oneself and others, and as an extra side benefit, a more relaxed and healthy body.

Why should we want to do this? Firstly, to relieve our own pain and suffering often caused by the confusion of not knowing who we really are. It may be helpful to establish that our first aim is to find a way of understanding or transforming our own pain and suffering, from there to find a way of relieving the suffering of others. If we are already dedicated to this goal but have not yet attended to our own needs, it is essential to remember that in order to give love or help to others we have to receive it ourselves, otherwise it is an empty gesture – a bankrupt cannot give generously of money he does not possess. When we truly receive and allow ourselves to be filled with love the experience can be so energizing that it spontaneously produces the wish to share that feeling with others. Effortless generosity is the fruit of such a practice.

Step One:
Meditation on Giving & Receiving:
(for understanding and healing relationships between oneself and others)

You've chosen the environment for your practice. You're sitting in a comfortable posture of your choice. You choose your motivation, e.g. you wish to relieve your own suffering.

Now choose an ideal of unconditional, pure compassionate love. If you belong to a specific religion and however you perceive God, use elements of this image as your model and guide, e.g. the forgiveness of Christ's love, the mother energy of the Virgin Mary, Tara, Shakti, Wakan Tanka (The Great Mystery) of the Native American tradition, or concentrate on the benefits of universal energy, the Mysterious Tao, or remember with gratitude how we are provided with support from our Universe, i.e. food, clothing, shelter, friends, relatives etc. If these fail to inspire, bring to mind the attributes of a living or historical role-model, e.g. the benevolence of Mother Teresa, Florence Nightingale, Gandhi, H.H. the Dalai Lama, or other religious or spiritual leaders.

As an alternative, consider more local or community-based personalities. Closer still, what about your grandparents, a favourite uncle or aunt or loving or inspirational friends. If that loving connection does not lie with an individual but with an environmental situation (a beach or forest, etc.) then imagine yourself sitting in that nourishing and inspirational setting.

Another suggestion is to look for a time in our lives when we felt loved and cherished by someone near to us and recognize that the capacity for receiving that love is still within.

Meditation practice:
for purifying the emotions
(obstacles to meditation)

Imagine the presence of the loving energy. On the in-breath, visualize or feel this energy centering into your heart. This can be in whatever form you feel comfortable, i.e. golden, white or rainbow light, or simply the feeling of warmth and compassion for oneself.

Allow it to mix with any physical pain or mental or emotional negativity which you long to cast off. Discharge this in the form of toxic smoke on the out-breath. If you find this difficult to visualize, then concentrate on the feeling of relief or release.

If you feel that you cannot easily visualize, imagine biting into a lemon and see if this stimulates an increase of saliva flow. Alternatively you could imagine the sound of fingernails screeching down a blackboard!

Continue in this way, receiving love and releasing any negativity, doubts or fears until such a time as there appears to be little or no difference between the in-breath and the out-breath.

It is not necessary to dwell on the physical mechanics of breathing as this could lead to hyper-ventilation taken to extremes. Conversely, it is quite common to find oneself spontaneously releasing mental, emotional or physical tension in the form of a deep sigh or involuntary body movements. As always, allow what is natural to occur without judgement or restriction. This, in itself, is a way of ensuring perfect equilibrium.

Step One can constitute a complete practice in its own right for the inability to receive love is a common imbalance in today's society. This may therefore be a helpful and simple way of practising healing for ourselves. How often have we been moved by the news of some disaster and felt powerless to help other than possibly on a financial level, thereby doing little to alleviate our own distress. An extension of this technique could be a helpful and simple way of sending healing energy to people we are concerned about, either on a personal level or in a wider context.

The following simple meditation can be an alternative or addition to Tong-Len at this stage.

Meditation on Kindness (Metta Bhavana):
As long as you can breathe, then you can do this practice. It doesn't involve elaborate preparation or complex mental gymnastics!

Breathing in: *Being energized.*
Breathing out: *Wishing others well.*

Meditation for Children
Breath Sunshine in,
Breath Clouds out.

Step Two: Tong-Len Meditation:
(for understanding and healing relationships between ourselves and others)

It can be observed in our day-to-day life that we have basic ways of relating to people, objects and circumstances which we could define as principle forms of reaction. We judge objects and people to be either 'good' or 'bad' in relation to ourselves. That which we deem unimportant we view with indifference. By using this practice it is possible to see the 'relative' nature of this view and how it could be the root cause of all our suffering. For

instance, we have all had the experience of being deeply attracted to an individual, even falling in love and, at some later date, disliking or hating them with equal intensity. The very qualities we initially found attractive are often the source of subsequent irritation. So let us examine the basic wishes of all living beings. We wish to be happy and free from suffering. We also wish to be loved unconditionally, free from judgement and limitation. In other words, to be accepted as we are. This meditational practice enables us to recognize this need in ourselves (Step One), and others (Step Two). This can transform many negative emotions and prejudices based on race, class, money, status etc., when we recognize our basic similarities instead of our differences. An excellent form of inter-cultural healing.

The Practice:
Choose three people who represent the following qualities:
a) **Someone you love**
b) **Someone to whom you are indifferent**
c) **Someone you dislike**

a) Someone you love
Visualize, or bring to mind, the person you have chosen and recognize that they are no different from youself. You both need love and freedom from suffering. Imagine that their suffering and pain has taken the form of a toxic or smokey cloud, surrounding them and obscuring your view. As you view them with sympathy and compassion you form the wish to take their pain from them and replace it with some of your own happiness.
Technique: On the in-breath, breathe this dark energy into your own heart, mix it and transform it into pure energy and on the out-breath return it as loving compassion. Continue with this practice until they appear smiling and happy. This is a gift from you to the person you love without conditions or desire for any reward other than their good health and well-being. This purifies possessive or selfish love. This is compassion!

b) Someone to whom you are indifferent
Select a person unknown to you personally (e.g. someone you may have seen passing in the street or on the TV news). This person should be someone who has neither harmed nor pleased you. Follow the same procedures as outlined in the previous technique. They are no different from yourself or the person you love. This will be your unexpected gift to them.

c) Someone you dislike
Initially, select a person whom you 'dislike' rather than hate, in order to build the practice up in easy steps. (This is really practising compassion on yourself!) A person you dislike is a person you have judged to be unacceptable in your world and you are attempting to push them away or deny their existence. By selecting them as a subject for your practice you are allowing yourself to suspend judgement and respect their right to be who they are. In other words, you like to be unconditionally accepted and you are prepared to extend this kindness to them. 'Re-spect' can be regarded as 'having a chance to look again'. Repeat the technique of taking their unhappiness and giving them your happiness in return.

You may well think this is the most difficult part of the practice. However, compare this with the pain of letting go of someone we love. There are usually only a very few people we passionately love or hate because the emotions take up so much energy. In comparison, how many other countless billions are there that we have not even thought about and to whose suffering we are indifferent: we will never be short of people who could benefit from our help in this area. This can be a way of transmuting or transforming our 'passion' into 'compassion' and become more loving and peaceful as a result of our understanding and commitment to change.

Our understanding is that we are no different from others. What we wish to receive as unconditional love, we practise giving. What we wish to give, we practise receiving. There is no difference. Balancing the two brings peace and equanimity. As our indifference to suffering diminishes, our ability to grow with love and awareness increases.

This practice enables us to clear up the emotional pollution that clouds our relationships bringing clarity and peace of mind which reduces mental and physical tension and serves to heal the conflict within ourselves. In the early stages we are removing the emotions we project onto others, creating a space for something positive to happen. We are acknowledging that we are creating our own suffering in the way that we relate to other beings and that we have the capacity to change.

We then have the choice between being overwhelmed by our emotions or transmuting them into a form of healing, connecting energy.

One way of coping with strong or unpleasant emotions is to discharge them. With Tong-Len, however, we can transform them from exhausting, destructive energy, to something we can actually utilize. Taking an alternative view of human or animal waste products, a farmer or gardener can transform something (viewed as 'bad') into compost (viewed as 'good'). In the East this process is regarded as using the transformative power of the emotions as fuel for enlightenment. In other words, there is no longer any need to fear the strength of our 'negative' emotions. They can be turned on their head to produce even greater insights.

Step Three: Tong-Len Meditation
(having compassion on oneself)
In order to prevent any unconscious retention of negative energies, return to Step One where you, once again, have the opportunity to receive unconditional love from your original source. This is a form of protection. As Shantideva says:

"Whoever wishes to quickly afford protection to both himself and others should practise that holy secret: the exchanging of self for others."

The meditation can be concluded by offering up the results or 'merit' of the practice to the benefit of all (sentient) beings. This unselfish dedication emphasizes our understanding that there is no difference between ourselves and others. Eventually, you may even be able to thank those with whom you were once angry for providing the incentive for you to initiate your own healing process.

Many stories abound in Tibet, of people with incurable diseases, e.g. leprosy, who took up this practice as a preparation for death. To their own astonishment and that of family and friends, they returned home after diligent practice, cured of their physical illness!

This core practice is also used for healing the mind, body and emotions and its role and application is discussed in *Easy Steps to Natural Healing*, a companion volume in the series.

Attachment, aversion and boredom
There are many things which can distract attention during meditation. Take noise, for example. Even after a place has been prepared where you would expect minimum distraction you may notice a noise creeping into your consciousness. Your reaction to it is based on how you 'judge' it. If you decide that it is 'unpleasant', then the noise will cause you suffering. Your negative emotions result from not accepting it as as mere sound, neither good nor bad. Suspend judgement, recognize your reaction as one of many other thoughts, let it go, and bring your mind home to the task in hand.

Conversely, an 'attractive' sound is another kind of noise, such as an unexpected burst of birdsong. Through our conditioning, we would tend to accept this as an attractive background addition to our meditational practice with its accompanying 'rewards' and blissful state. Recognize your perception of this as 'just a thought' and a manifestation of our habitual addiction to 'good' feelings'. This is a pleasant distraction but a distraction nonetheless. It is an intrinsic need within ourselves to feel we must ascribe different qualities to what simply 'is' or exists in its own right. If we become attached to the birdsong, we could suffer a sense of loss when it eventually ceases. So, let go of this thought, return to the practice and . . .

DO IT AGAIN!

Boredom and Ennui (indifference)
This is a defence mechanism that comes into play when we get close to the truth as a result of meditation: a cessation of grasping or attachment to 'good thoughts' and a pushing away or aversion to 'bad thoughts'. This sometimes results in a mixture of apathy, fear and

disenchantment, a kind of limbo or no-man's land. This state is not so much one of equanimity or equilibrium but of suspended animation. The energetic dynamic between the polarities has been arrested, not balanced.

Bliss State, Fear State

These are strong emotions generally thought of as respectively 'positive' and 'negative'. To the meditator there is no difference between these and feelings of boredom. They are equal distractions within any form of discipline. These states can be transmuted in a practice such as Tong-Len (see page 39). However, in 'awareness meditation' it is sufficient to know that it becomes an obstacle if you wrestle with them, either to embrace them or to push them away. The powerful waves of bliss can be overwhelmingly attractive. A great Catholic mystic warned those who would indulge in this state that they risked becoming like 'bees caught in their own honey'.

As meditation deepens, so does the intensity of our experience of these emotional states. Far from being an indication that we are poor at meditation, this can indicate how close we are to recognizing a truer state of mind. When these obstacles appear, and we are prepared to simply continue with the practice, they can bring to light our hidden resources and deepen our commitment. These so-called 'bad experiences' are merely the uncovering of yet another layer of the mind. Use them as a basis for the next stage of practice or, alternatively, continue to observe the rising emotions, recognizing them as just intangible, illusory thoughts' and let them go. In other words, return to your practice and . . .
DO IT AGAIN!

Doubts & Reservations

The initial feelings of awareness to come to the surface, through the focus of one-pointed meditation or concentration, will make you realize just how mentally undisciplined you are. The mind at this stage has been variously described as 'monkey mind' or 'unbroken horse' and compared to a 'rudderless ship' adrift on a sea of confusion. Meditational practices are aimed at 'taming the wild mind-flow'. Commitment to training and tuning the mind is of tantamount importance, just as an athlete or dancer trains the body.

Although this may seem daunting, all that is necessary at first is to practise for a short time each day. Devote as much time as you can manage, and don't try to compete with yourself (the antithesis of meditation). After a while, your practice will become habitual, but a useful habit rather than an unhelpful one. A classic image is that of a pot which fills, little by little, a drop at a time, until it is full.

If at this time you feel that you still don't know enough, perhaps this story will inspire you. The fame of a legendary meditation master reached the ears of a learned professor. He arranged a meeting with the Master and, while waiting for him to serve the traditional tea, told him of his position at the University and his years of concentrated study. The Master smiled amiably while pouring the tea into the professor's cup. As the professor continued to regale him with his accomplishments, the Master continued to pour tea into an already full cup. The professor pointed this out with astonishment. The Master looked at him and said: *You are like this cup, full to overflowing. Until you empty yourself I am unable to give you anything."*

So, if you are a beginner, congratulations, you have an empty cup. This state of consciousness is known as 'Zen Mind, Beginner's Mind' and indicates the freshness and openness of a humble mind.

Benefits of Meditation

The physical body takes a time to reach a peak of condition and strength so, in all probability, it will take time to experience the benefits of regular meditation. If you expect a golden chariot to sweep you off to the heavens and rescue you from yourself, you may be disappointed! Perhaps, with every new insight, you hope to be greeted with a roar of approval from the hosts of cosmic beings about you. It might happen, but then again it may not. The expectation that enlightenment will suddenly occur in a 'blaze of glory' is a tricky belief and may hinder progress. Our understanding often comes as a painful realization of our own ignorance. All too often, the very practices designed to liberate us can chain us to a misguided ideal which we can't live up to. The following Zen *koan* is a paradoxical riddle about the nature of existence or eternal truth. Koans are given by spiritual masters to educate their students to free themselves from their mental preconceptions.

"What is the sound of one hand clapping?"

This is a source of contemplation rather than an intellectual conundrum. However, this did not prevent the publication of a book offering Westerners 100 koans and their answers! The koans are designed to shock the conditioned mind out of old dualistic forms of thinking by presenting it with seemingly unsolvable questions. The benefits lie in the process of realization, not in the 'answer'. After realization, the Zen Master simply gives the student another appropriate koan. Similarly, in our meditational practice, realizations and insights will arise. Try to avoid the need to share your discoveries with all and sundry: let them go and settle back into your regular meditational practice.

St. John of the Cross observed: *"He who interrupts the course of his spiritual exercises and prayer is like a man who allows a bird to escape from his hand: he can hardly catch it again."*

To obtain the greatest benefit from regular practice, realize that ten minutes of quality, committed meditation is better than an hour of dutiful or unfocused practice. Choose a time and duration to which you can commit yourself without feeling you are neglecting other areas of your life. Make it a daily requirement, a 'good' habit such as brushing your teeth. When you start to feel the benefits you will not begrudge your commitment.

"There's only one failure in meditation – the failure to meditate."

Waking Up the Mind

In the early morning, after a good night's sleep, get up immediately. Experience shows that 'dozing' for that extra hour is often counter-productive. Your consciousness slides confusedly between the two distinct states of waking and dreaming. A practice called 'Dream Yoga' could enable you to take your awareness with you into sleep time, utilizing the lucid state in order to extend your spiritual practices. This is an advanced practice for adepts but, for most of us, it is sufficient to 'wake up' in our 'daytime' dream and progress from there.

One of the side benefits of regular meditation is to decrease the amount of sleep required. This makes, "I'd like to meditate but I haven't

Taking the Benefits into your Daily Life

Once you have a basic understanding of the simple principles involved, you will be eager to grasp any opportunity of filling the natural spaces which appear in any full and busy day. Just recognize these 'gaps' which occur between your everyday chores and relax into them. This can include such simple things as walking in a park, making tea, sitting quietly with awareness, etc. St. Thérèse de Lisieux gave absolute and minute attention to everyday tasks confirming the importance of every second in what she called her 'little way'.

Meditation can intensify negative traits as well as bringing welcome benefits. This can occur after concentrated practice when you relax back into an everyday situation. Try to take your awareness with you and be alert to subtle or dramatic changes in lifestyle, attitudes and experiences. The purification of 'unhealthy' states of mind may produce a temporary effect similar to the 'healing crisis' experienced during a physical detoxification process.

As you may well expect to read this once again (with increased compassion) return to your practice and . . .

DO IT AGAIN!

Consistent practice in such arts as single-pointedness, or any exercise in concentration, enables you to learn to do one thing at a time. In meditation we reduce the tendency for the mind to skip about between this and that. If your attention is not also 'mindful' of what you are doing there will be a split focus and the mind's dualis-

tic nature will still be apparent. While engaged in everyday tasks, you should be aware that whatever you are doing you can also experience it more directly by cultivating an attitude of mindfulness. When doing something, just do it. As a result, the simplicity of the famous Zen saying: "When I eat, I eat. When I sleep, I sleep" becomes less obscure and more about our ordinary human life.

Following this observation, we can say "When I meditate, I meditate." We simply do it, paradoxically, without expectations. The following Zen aphorisms illustrate the process of enlightenment along this journey into supreme consciousness.

> *"Before enlightenment*
> *gathering twigs*
> *carrying water.*
> *After enlightenment*
> *gathering twigs*
> *carrying water."*

This koan illustrates the point that meditation does not take you to some 'other-worldly' place. You stay truly within yourself. You may still carry on the daily tasks and routines of your current everyday life but you will bring a new awareness to them so that they become subtly different. Your consciousness will grow in awareness and the most mundane of acts will take on a new significance.

> *"To a beginner on the Path*
> *A tree is a tree,*
> *a mountain is a mountain.*
> *To one who is treading the path,*
> *a tree is no longer a tree,*
> *a mountain no longer a mountain!*
> *To one who has realized the Path*
> *A tree is once more a tree,*
> *a mountain once more a mountain."*

By cultivating an open view you can expect the unexpected: without restrictions you can achieve the true benefits of meditation which are limitless. No beginning, no end. In our ignorance we strayed onto the Path for in the presence of Pure Natural Mind there is no Path, no Journey . . .

WE ARE ALREADY HOME!

got time" rather an invalid excuse. Meditation can provide you with the extra time you need!

Meditation is all about BEING IN THE HERE AND NOW, not in the future or past, not in a trance, not in the middle of some romantic 'space opera' loading ourselves with distractions rather than bravely confronting the all-powerful NOW. You may have heard or used the phrase: "The lights are on, but there is nobody at home". Meditation is a way of coming home.

Do I need a Meditation Teacher?

The answer is, 'almost certainly', at least at some stage. I'm sure there must be cases where devotees have learnt all there is to know from a book, but it's not just about learning techniques. The profound psychological changes brought about by such powerful techniques can be literally life-changing and a whole host of questions are likely to arise: "Am I doing the practice correctly? What do I do if I find myself suddenly swamped by anger/fear/jealousy, etc? As constantly reiterated, the answer simply lies in returning to the practice and doing it again. However, religious/spiritual systems are a treasure-house of practical knowledge about such matters and are inhabited by people just like you who are practising and in many cases having experiences which parallel your own. To ignore all that potential guidance would be unwise.

The Yoga tradition of India has a term, *Satsang*, which broadly translated means 'fellowship with truth' (also implying the search after truth). In the early stages of meditation you are like a young sapling, subject to harsh winds, blown in many directions. Yet if you choose to associate with like-minded people who aspire to useful meditation (other saplings) you are together less susceptible to damage, especially in those vulnerable early stages of experience.

Most traditions of religion and belief either accept or would insist upon practice in conjunction with teachers and other students as one of the most important prerequisites in the quest for spiritual growth. This is certainly true of the major religions; Christians and Jews congregate to pray, contemplate and meditate, Muslims in a mosque, Hindus in temples and Buddhists have the concept of *Sangha*,, the Vajrayana path,for instance, insisting that the presence of a teacher is essential.

What to Look For in a Teacher

If you decide to look for a teacher, look first to personal recommendation. If you don't know anyone who practises meditation, go to your public library and look for lists of groups and organizations.

You would do well to consider the following points when evaluating a potential teacher or group:

- Is the teacher, method or group in sympathy with your deepest goals and general disposition? Be wary of any that seek to deny your highest aspirations.

- Be wary of any person or group demanding large sums of money up front before being prepared to reveal any of their precious teachings.

- Does the teacher personally embody the benefits claimed to result from their method. Are they compassionate, calm, understanding and tolerant.

- Is the teacher committed to their method/path and do they communicate clearly?

- Is the teacher more concerned about their goals than yours?

- Does the teacher spontaneously respond to your needs and do they inspire and instil confidence in your ability to stand on your own two feet.

- A teacher should be a true 'spiritual friend' who will serve to mirror your 'good' and 'bad' qualities. When you get to the point where you genuinely wish to follow a spiritual path, you must be willing to accept both.

- Remember, the beauty and wisdom you see in any teacher is but a reflection of those qualities which exist in youself.

In any teacher-student relationship, it is difficult to follow the true spiritual approach and not fall into the trap of habitual over-expectation. In the beginning, you should rely on your natural instincts and not dwell too deeply on the whys and wherefores of your choice – follow your feelings.

THE FINAL NOTE

As meditation deepens, emotions, cravings, compulsions and fears begin to lose their energy and power over us. In this new climate of openness choice is now a possibility. So, why not liberate yourself from addictive habits and negative behaviour by recognizing them for what they are and choosing not to be controlled by them. We are empowered with the ability to live more positively, with free will, as God and our true natures intended.

Buddha said: *"All that we are is a result of what we have thought"*. By changing our *modus operandi* (way of operating), we change our habit of conditioned thinking and thereby change ourselves.

Relative Belief
"Meditation is the Activity of 'Doing' and the Ultimate View is the Activity of 'Being.' "

It must be admitted that any opinions or viewpoints expressed in this book are relative and subject to amendment. None of them are solid truths, set in stone. We have to be more open and flexible than that. Hopefully, some of the ideas will give you a taste for meditation and a different perspective on the subject of human existence.

What we offer here is our highest truth as we see it. By embracing and accepting it we have exposed ourselves to the possibility of developing a more expanded view, and you must learn to do the same. If we pretend to be the guardians of knowledge we do not in fact possess, we only serve to arrest our own spiritual growth and this is not a useful activity. All we can work with is our truth as we perceive it. We take part in the activity and engage in the business of it. Everything else is a mere distraction.

Ultimate View

During meditation, when confusion arises, recognize its 'relative' nature, relax and allow it to resolve into the 'Absolute'. Rediscover and rest in your sky-like nature.

> "Rest in natural great peace
> This exhausted mind
> Beaten helplessly by karma*
> And neurotic thought
> Like the relentless fury of pounding waves
> in the infinite ocean of Samsara."**

* *karma* – the law of cause and effect
**Samsara – the world of suffering and delusion

Text by Nyoshul Khen Rinpoche from *Songs of Experience*, Rigpa, London, 1989.

A Simple Truth

You already know all you need to know about meditation. It is so simple that you will find it difficult to grasp this fundamental idea – to be what you already are! This book will help you complicate things and either satisfy your need to be elaborate or make you so tired of the complexities that you'll be willing to drop your resistence to relaxing into your natural state of being.

So, stop right here. Look directly into your mind and . . .

BE HERE IN NOW

RECOMMENDED READING

The Tibetan Book of Living and Dying
by Sogyal Rinpoche.

Relative World, Ultimate Mind
The Twelfth Tai Situpa.

Living Deliberately
by Harry Palmer.

Meditations from the Tantras
by Paramahansa Satyananda.

Yoga Nidra
by Paramahansa Satyananda.

The Myth of Freedom
by Chogyam Trungpa.

How to Meditate
by Lawrence LeShan.

I Ching – or Book of Changes
translated by Richard Wilhelm.

Tai Chi Ch'uan – The Technique of Power
by Tem Horwitz & Susan Kimmelman
with H.H. Lui.

T'ai Chi Ch'uan and Meditation
by Da Liu.

Journey into Consciousness
by Charles Breaux .

Way to Go
by Khentin Tai Situ Pa

*Meditation – Commonsense Directions
or an Uncommon Life*
by Eknath Easwaran.

Yoga Made Easy
by Rosalind Widdowson.

Easy Steps to Natural Healing
by Rosalind Widdowson.

*How To Know God –
The Yoga Aphorisms of Patanjali*
by Swami Prabhavananda
& Christopher Isherwood

*Passages – A Guide for Pilgrims
of the Mind*
by Marianne S. Anderson
& Louis M. Savary

Awakening the Spine
by Vanda Scaravelli.